DEAR GOD,
I HAVE THIS
TERRIBLE PROBLEM...
A Housewife's Secret Letters

Bernadette McCarver Snyder

LIGUORI
PUBLICATIONS

One Liguori Drive
Liguori, Missouri 63057
(314) 464-2500

Imprimi Potest:
John F. Dowd, C.SS.R.
Provincial, St. Louis Province
Redemptorist Fathers

Imprimatur:
Monsignor Edward J. O'Donnell
Vicar General, Archdiocese of St. Louis

ISBN-0-89243-188-1
Library of Congress Catalog Card Number: 83-81511

Cover Design: Pam Hummelsheim

<u>from *The House and Home,* 1896</u>

"No woman — so far as one can judge from printed collections — ever wrote more pleasant letters than do the American women. " . . . when they are natural, they are best. They dress up little nothings with infinite drollery."

<u>from MY house and home, 1983</u>

I share these letters in the hope that I have dressed up my little nothings with enough drollery to give you a smile, a pleasant moment, and maybe even a closer friendship with the one who signs his letters "God."
With humility and awe, I ask his forgiveness if I have been disrespectful in quoting him or careless in misquoting him.

Bernadette McCarver Snyder

With love, I dedicate this little book to my little mother — cute, darlin', joyful, sweet, happy Hazel Davids McCarver — who taught me to talk to God . . . and to expect an answer!

Dear God,

I have this terrible problem. My car has a death wish.

Last week I was running late as usual and my gas gauge was running low as usual — so I screeched into a station, pulled up to the self-service pump, leaped out, and clumsily managed to get the gas into the car, feeling very self-sufficient and independent.

I even remembered to check the price, see that the charge ticket was filled out correctly, and write down my mileage. Then, in a spurt of zealous conscientiousness, I took time to drive through the automatic car wash.

There was only one thing I forgot, God. I forgot to put the cap back on the gas tank. I forgot to do that, God, BEFORE I went through the car wash.

Do you realize, God, that I am probably the only one in town with laundered gasoline and a waxed fuel pump?

Why didn't my car warn me? It could have honked its horn, refused to start, or SOMETHING. Surely it realized that its engine is probably allergic to detergent!

5

A week later, while I was still expecting the car to cough, then roll over on its back in the middle of a busy highway, it got thirsty again. That's another thing, God — this car definitely has a drinking problem.

Anyway, I figured I'd better not try self-service again, so I brazenly pulled up to the full-service pump. The young man who served that pump would have made a turtle look faster than a speeding bullet. He FINALLY figured out how to pump the gas into my detergent-clogged tank, checked the oil, and announced that my car was thirsty for that, too. Exasperated (as usual), I looked at my watch and realized I was definitely going to be late for the meeting I had expected to make right on time.

When it seemed the young man had finished everything, he took my charge card and started writing out the ticket. There was just one thing — he had not closed the hood of my car. Hoping to SUBTLY impress on him that I was in a hurry, I started the engine.

This got his attention. He said quickly (for the first time), "Please turn off the engine, lady." It seems he had NOT forgotten to close the hood. It was still open because he had not removed the oil can. YOU KNOW what happened, don't you, God? Oil all over the engine, the sides of the car, etc., etc. I leaped out and helped the newly energetic young man try to mop it up with paper towels, but it didn't do much good. My car just sat there and smirked, knowing that it had further managed to endanger its health.

What should I do, God? Will this car and I ever manage to make it down the highway of life together?

Worried

Dear Worried,

I'm glad I finally got your attention. I've been wanting to speak to you about your Automobile Etiquette — but it isn't easy to be heard above the roar of your motor (not your car's motor — YOURS). You really shouldn't always be in such a hurry that you

6

have to SCREECH into stations. Skip a few of those meetings and spend the time visiting with me. We have a LOT to talk about.

And on the highway — instead of going over the speed limit and spending all your time watching for ticket-toting policemen, slow down and watch for ME. I'm there. I'm the little boy who waves to you from the back of a pickup truck, hoping you'll take time to wave back. I'm the cluster of trees on the hillside and the clouds on the horizon. I'm the patch of wild flowers that bloom right by the side of the highway you travel every day. I'm the hitchhiker who reminds you how lucky you are to be traveling in air-cooled or wind-cooled comfort while he thumbs in the sun. I'm there — if you'll look for me. I'm listening — if you'll talk to me. I'm ready to help — if you'll follow my road signs.

Don't worry, Worried. On the highway of life I'm with you. How could I miss you — you're the only one traveling in a car that has a motor with soapsuds on the inside and oil on the outside.

God

Dear God,

Do you remember those old movies about the dust bowl out West somewhere — where clouds of dust blew in and covered everything? It has moved into my house.

In fact, I think my son's best friend is a dust ball. It started living under his bed some time ago — and then it moved its whole family into his room. Now there are dust balls behind, under, and next to everything in there. He begs me not to vacuum, saying he is afraid I will destroy some of those valuable tiny scraps of paper that have all his school notes scribbled on them. But I know the truth. One vacuuming would wipe out his friend's whole family.

But it doesn't stop there, God. It's an epidemic that spreads through the house the minute you close an eyelid. I can start dusting in the front room and by the time I have moved through the house and put away the dust cloth, the dastardly dust has re-appeared in the front room and a big, fat dust ball has already claimed squatter's rights under the sofa.

What should I do, God? Am I doomed to dust detail forever?

Defeated

Dear Defeated,

The dust you will always have with you. I hate to mention this, but I made the dust too. It must have seemed like a good idea at the time. I hope you don't let this affect our friendship.

Don't be discouraged by the dust, Defeated. Try dusting less and enjoying it more. Pretend it's an exercise to help you lose weight. Pretend dust is an alien invader and only you can save the universe by destroying it — or at least delaying it.

Try dusting only half as much as you do now — and see if anybody notices. Then use the extra time you save to enjoy the good things I made — the daisies and the dewdrops, the daffodils and the Dalmatians, the deer and the dear, the dandelions (oops . . . I shouldn't have mentioned those . . .).

God

Dear God,

I have this terrible problem. I have lost the will to cook.

I didn't realize it until yesterday when I saw a cartoon in the funny page. The lady was sitting at her kitchen table, looking dejectedly at a cookbook, and she was saying: "I have lost the will to cook." I knew immediately that I had identified my problem.

How did this happen, Lord? Remember when I was a young bride and started collecting cookbooks instead of Hummels? While all my friends were reading trashy novels, I was reading wholesome cookbooks. And where did it get me? Twenty pounds overweight — that's where!

Everybody who comes to our house raves about my wonderful cooking, but the people who LIVE here couldn't care less. My husband's idea of a gourmet meal is hotdogs and beans. He raves when I serve that. But when I serve Boeuf a la Mystery Sauce — or some recipe that has taken three hours to prepare and every measuring spoon in the house to add ⅛ of a teaspoon of this spice and ⅜ of a spoonful of that condiment — THEN the first thing he does is pour pepper over it and ask, "What kind of stew is this?"

And my son is just as bad. He thinks a good homemade cookie is one you buy at the door from a Girl Scout. Homemade soup that has been simmered lovingly all day is an ordeal for him, but he LIKES plain old canned soup. And HIS idea of a gourmet meal is a TV dinner.

Is it any wonder my passion for pots and pans has paled, my enthusiasm for souffles has fallen, the thrill has gone from trussing a turkey or poaching a pear? Dear God, what am I going to do with those two hundred cookbooks I've carefully collected, the sixty-three varieties of spices, the special recipes in my special file, and the sign that says, "Caution: Trespassers will be fed"?

Hungry for Comfort

Dear Hungry for Comfort,

A family does not live by bread alone — even if it IS homemade. Give them hotdogs and cold, store-bought cookies. Give *yourself* some time to read, to pray, to sit by the window and enjoy my sunsets and morning glories, to discover the patterns in my clouds, to listen to my birds and to what I want you to hear.

And on those days when the "will to cook" threatens to return, make up a special recipe and take dinner to someone who is lonely or blue. OR whip up your souffles and sorbets, your quiche and croissants, and invite some ladies in for lunch. They deserve the break, and you do too. And who knows — maybe your family will begin to miss those gourmet goodies — and you can start the pots and pans simmering and stewing again instead of your temper.

In the meantime, remember that I am the one who made the carrots and chickens, the onions and potatoes — AND the chocolate — so that someone like you would enjoy them. And I am proud of you for using the talent I gave you for turning them into incredible edibles.

God

Dear God,

Sorry I'm late with this letter — but then I owe my mother-in-law a letter, too . . . and my sister and my cousin and my nephew. . . . Well, you know how my good intentions suffer from bad follow-through.

In fact, that's what I wanted to write you about . . . that bad follow-through. For years, I've been planning to clean out the closets, arrange my spices in alphabetical order, organize the pantry, and do something with the pots and pans so they won't all fall out every time I open the cabinet door. I have also planned to take a Speed Reading Course, learn to play the piano, and sew up that little rip in the hem of my black skirt so I can take out the safety pin.

Somehow I haven't found time to do any of those things. What's the matter with me, Lord?

People in magazines and on soap operas always find time to do those things. I haven't seen one yet with a safety pin in the hem of her skirt.

I read an article by an efficiency expert who said you should start organizing by breaking down your day into fifteen-minute segments and writing down what you do. I tried that, but every day all the fifteen-minute segments had something different in them, and it took so long to write down all the stuff I had to organize that the laundry started seeping under the basement door, the "chores undone" list got longer than it ever had before, and we ran out of bread and milk. We also ran out of paper and pencils and aspirin because I had used them all up trying to put together the organization chart.

The expert also said that it is inefficient to let "other people" waste your time. But God, the "other people" on my chart are the ones I love and WANT to waste time with. What should I do?

Belated

Dear Belated,

I HAVE noticed that your follow-through is not as good as your put-off, get-around, and wait-until-tomorrow. All organization is not ornery. You might look at that chart again and consider all the things that you could probably do in half the time — if you didn't spend most of the time dreading doing them and putting them off and worrying about when you are going to do them and wondering how you could do them faster.

Don't spend so much time BEFORE each chore wondering how and when you can do it . . . and then time AFTER wondering if you did it right or could have done it differently. Just do it and forget it.

But I know it IS difficult in today's hurry-hurry world to get everything done. Maybe you could leave out a few of the things in your life without leaving out any of the people.

And when things get too bad, just call for my help. I'm busy too — but never too busy to help *you*.

God

Dear God,

Do you know that name-droppers have been dropping your name on everything from pillows to plaques, from bumper stickers to balloons — and even beyond?

Cleanliness used to be next to godliness — but now I think it must be CERAMICS! Everything that could have possibly been made out of ceramics has been made with your name on it.

Slogans range from "God bless this mess" to "God loves Grandma's little angel." (Sometimes they're the same: Grandma's little angel is a mess or made the mess!)

Even Hollywood used your name in a movie called *Oh God* — and it was so successful they had to make a sequel.

Do you mind our using your name so freely this way, God? Do you mind seeing your name spelled out in sparklers on the 4th of July, in sequins on a dayglow T-shirt, in the dust on the back of a pickup truck?

Do you like "God Bless America" being thrown around freely by people who haven't spoken to you in years? What do you think about "God loves a jogger" or "God hates a quitter"? And how do you feel about "Honk if you love Jesus"?

Name Withheld

Dear Name Withheld,

I must confess it was a bit unsettling when I first saw my name on mugs, jugs, and VW bugs. It may not be quite as holy as it could be, but at least my name is with the people — and that's where I've always wanted to be.

Maybe those who haven't spoken to me in years will be reminded of who and what I am . . . maybe the message will get through subliminally and eventually. Maybe they will even want to renew our acquaintance.

My ways are not the world's ways, so I might wish the messages were a little more meaningful or in good taste — but some of my best apostles were not too subtle either. So don't worry, Name Withheld, it's nice to see my name in lights — or even ceramic. Remember — it pays to advertise!

God

Dear God,

Did you know that according to an apothecaries' measure, one scruple equals twenty grains . . . and three scruples equal one dram? Well of course you knew that — you know everything. But I don't . . . and that's why I'm writing you.

It seems to me, Lord, that recently scruples about right and wrong are being taken with a grain of salt and nobody gives a dram!

When the first few "shocking" television series came on the air, I refused to watch them and even wrote letters of disapproval. But then a few little "shocking" bits appeared in our regular favorite shows. Since it was just an occasional happening, we said "tch, tch" and overlooked it. Gradually, more and more slipped in, and we didn't even notice anymore. We had been desensitized!

Once upon a time "soap operas" were appropriately named because the heroes and heroines were squeaky clean, their characters never besmirched by even a hint of anything dirty. Today, all the "soaps" do is air their dirty laundry! And no one even says "tch, tch" anymore. Everyone just laughs about everything hateful, spiteful, and even evil that the stars depict as real life. And they don't want to miss a single episode for fear they might not get all the dirt.

Where will it all end, Lord? The magazines that used to be sold only in "dirty bookstores" are now sold at the counters where our children go to buy candy bars. The books that are best sellers and are reviewed in newspapers, discussed on talk shows, and displayed at the library don't hesitate to detail every possible sort of deviant and sinful behavior.

Did I say "sinful"? Goodness, who uses that word anymore? What IS a sin, Lord? All the things we used to think were sins have suddenly become "games people play." Sodom and Gomorrah are beginning to sound like Fun City. And my conscience is so confused; I am afraid it has had a breakdown!

What can I do, God? I don't want to have too many scruples, but I think I should have more than a few grains worth!

Confused

Dear Confused,

You are not alone. Many of my "good" people are not too sure how much it takes to be good today.

I wanted everyone to be good out of love, not fear. But then the word LOVE got misused and abused. Now no one seems to remember its true meaning. Just be careful, Confused. I don't want you to be scrupulous about every little thing — like when you were a child and hippity-hopped down the sidewalk for fear "if you step on a crack, you'll break your mother's back!"

Just remember the old rules for sin — serious matter, full reflection, and complete consent of the will. It has to be serious and you have to think about it carefully and then decide that you want to do it even if it's bad.

The people who think sin and evil have gone out of style are even more confused than you are. This is a true absence of love. So don't be scrupulous — but keep a *few* scruples because I still give a dram.

God

Dear God,

I have this terrible problem. I just read my horoscope for the day, and it says I was born under a bad sign — a flashing yellow light. It doesn't come out and say I am cowardly, but that does seem to be a not-very-subtle hint. It cautions me to stay out of falling elevators and tells me not to try having a meaningful relationship with potted plants. What kind of horoscope is that?

It does have one thing noted accurately though. My horoscope says that I am the kind of person who spends a lot of time sitting around hoping, tossing coins into fountains and wells, and wishing on a star.

That's true, God. It started when I was about sixteen and never let up. I am an incurable hoper. I keep hoping I will win a sweepstakes, a beauty contest, or a free car wash. I'm not particular.

I hope the red light will turn green before I get there, the mailman will bring something besides bills, or my hair will look right just once on a day when I am going somewhere besides the grocery. Yes, I am addicted to hope.

I am a little too cowardly to turn the yellow to green and go out and MAKE something happen. But I always hope it will. How can I turn this hope into cope?

Waiting

Dear Waiting,

Hope is a virtue — and I'm glad you have it — but it CAN be carried too far. Maybe it's time for you to stop tossing coins and start turning corners.

Be brave enough to start trying to make a few things happen without just waiting for them to fall into your lap. Start with something small; and if you fall on your face the first time and come up looking like a fool, don't let it stop you. I will be there for you to cry on my shoulder. Just pick yourself up and start over, HOPING that the next time it will work out better.

Hope is the crocus blooming in a snowstorm, promising spring. Don't lose it. But don't spend your life wishing and waiting for something to happen. There is too much work to be done; there are too many songs to be sung. My work and my songs.

God

Dear God,

I am in a lot of trouble. I can't speak computer.

When this machine moved into our spare bedroom, I had no idea it was going to make me an outcast in my own family.

My son sits down in front of it and his fingers fly over the keyboard, and he and the computer communicate. They say things like "ROM . . . BRUN . . . Integer BASIC . . . GOSUB . . . DOS Command . . . BLOAD." Is that any way to talk in front of a mother?

Then my husband addresses the computer. He tells it all his football statistics, and it gobbles them up and stores them away secretly in its memory bank. Then it hums and smirks, knowing how much he loves football and knowing that he will be back later so they can have long talks together about it. My husband never talks to me that way!

Now everywhere I look — books, magazines, television — all I see and hear is "computer . . . computer." Everyone's selling or talking computer — and I still don't speak the language.

What should I do, God? I tried reading the instruction book, but just the Table of Contents scared me to death. It listed things like "Altering the Microprocessor Registers . . . Accessing the Mini-Assembler . . . Eight-Bit Binary Arithmetic . . . Program Optimization . . . Booting the Disk." See what I mean? Booting the Disk sounds a little like football — maybe that's why my husband is getting such a boot out of it and why I would like to GIVE it the boot! Dear God, I think this computer has put the byte on us!

Rotten Apple

Dear Rotten Apple,

I know progress can be irritating. I have certainly had to put up with a lot of it. Leonardo da Vinci was always coming up with some newfangled idea, and since then it's just been one new thing after another here on earth. (I've even had to put up with new-fangled ideas in the Church!)

But be patient. Progress may be painful, but it IS necessary. Computers are just the next step for your generation. Your parents might have wondered why you needed television when you already had radio, and their parents probably thought it would be easier to go on hitching up the horse instead of learning to drive a car. So now it's your turn.

Instead of spending so much time with your old-fashioned things — driving your car and watching your television — sign up to take a computer course somewhere. Once you learn to speak the language, you might get a boot out of computer disks too! You might discover that they can help you organize your household accounts or your recipes — or even that storeroom in your basement. Heaven knows you could use some organization there!

So byte the bullet and learn computer. An apple a day just might make you healthy — or even wealthy and wise!

God

Dear God,

I would love to be a television news reporter, but I can't. I have crooked teeth.

Why is it, God, that the only way we can get the news anymore is through a set of terrific teeth? The reports we get may be slanted, poorly researched, downright inaccurate, or just plain boring — but the reporters smile so brightly through it all you'd think they owned stock in a toothpaste company!

Why is it, God, that we can't have a plain, old, kind-of-ugly reporter with crooked teeth and a definite overbite, so we could feel comfortable watching him tell us about natural disasters, fires, floods, murders, and muggings? It's embarrassing hearing things like that coming from the beautiful mouths of the beautiful people!

And speaking of that bad news, why does the news always have to be bad? Can't we hear some good news sometime? And what about the truth? Where can we find it? Every reporter tells a different version of the same story. How do we know which one to believe? Maybe we would find it easier to believe if we could ever find a reporter with some kind of background qualifications other than just a good dentist!

Not Smiling

Dear Not Smiling,

A lot of people feel just like you do — they're not smiling through today's kind of news. And I KNOW you don't have to have good teeth to be a good reporter. None of my apostles had terrific teeth — but they all did a terrific job of reporting MY news . . . and it was GOOD news and it was the truth.

But don't be too hard on the Beautiful People either. You don't have to be ugly to be talented or truthful. Some of the good-looking reporters also look good to me because they ARE trying to face the truth and the consequences of today's news. But YOU have a job to do too. You have to do some reading and research on your own so you will be knowledgeable enough to recognize the truth when you see it.

And you also have a responsibility to be a good reporter in your own backyard — even if you do have bad teeth. Truth begins at home; so when you tell a story, watch out for the embroidery! I have noticed that some of the stories YOU have passed on have been a bit slanted and poorly researched too (not to mention downright inaccurate or just plain boring).

And you must concentrate on the GOOD news too. Don't pass on bad news you hear about friends and neighbors — keep that to yourself. But when there's good news, spread it as thick as you can. And when there's no good news, do something to MAKE good news. Then, Not Smiling, you can start smiling — and make your whole little piece of the world smile with you!

God

Dear God,

The Russians are coming. And they're messing up my back-yard.

You see, before we moved into this house, somebody planted some Russian olive trees near the back door right next to the patio. And now I know just how a witch feels! Because of those trees, I spend half my time with a broomstick in my hands.

In the spring, the trees get these lovely little yellow flowers on them. But then the flowers start falling, and I have to sweep them up. No matter how often I sweep, every time I look out on the patio there are more to be swept up.

Then the trees get covered with beautiful green leaves that are so thick they shade the patio and make it look like an oasis of green. There's only one problem: Russian olive trees have a strange habit of dropping leaves all the time — even right in the middle of summer. So I have to sweep them up. No matter how often I sweep, every time I look out on the patio, there are more to be swept up.

Then when it's about half-past summer, the Russian "olives" appear — little green things that the birds love to eat. The only thing is that the birds don't eat them all, so the olives start falling onto the patio — and if you step on them, they squish and make a stain. So I have to sweep them up. No matter how often I sweep, every time I look out on the patio, there are more to be swept up.

The worst time of all is fall. Then the leaves fall faster than ever and so do all the leftover olives. And you know what I have to do — double duty with the broom.

And no matter how MUCH I sweep, I never do get them all by the first snowfall, so they sort of meld together into a mulch around the patio. Then when the snow melts I have to scoop off all those meshed-together leaves so the flowers can start coming up; and as soon as I've finished that — you've guessed it! The little yellow flowers start coming out, and it's time to get the broom again.

What should I do, God? I really didn't plan to spend my life stuck to a broomstick!

Up a Tree

Dear Up a Tree,

Well, it looks like you'll have to find a way to fight those Russians! Maybe you could stop worrying so much about how the patio looks and, no matter what, only sweep once a week — or when company's coming! OR instead of whistling while you work, speak while you sweep. Make your cleanup-patio time into prayer time. While you sweep, recite some memorized prayers you learned as a child or sing some hymns or just meditate on all the wonderful things in the world — like blossoms in the springtime, cool shade in the summer, a banquet for the birds, and mulch for the winter! Can you think of anything that provides ALL those things — anything in your own backyard?

They say that you have to ''cultivate a taste'' for olives, but once you like them you love them. Maybe the same is true with Russian olive trees.

God

Dear God,

Last week my teenager was sick with a cold — and it was sickening! He moaned like he had bubonic plague and issued orders like he was Chief of Staff of the Armed Forces. He expected round-the-clock nursing, meals a la carte, and tender loving care beyond the call of motherhood. His slight case of the flu made me fly off the handle!

The second morning he announced that it was the end of the quarter at his school, and he had two reports that absolutely HAD to be turned in to two different teachers that day or it would totally destroy his entire high school record. I mentioned his case of bubonic plague and asked if that wouldn't excuse him . . . but he said BOTH teachers had emphatically declared that NO excuses would be acceptable.

It was snowing that morning, and I was due to leave for a meeting at 9:30; but I dashed around and got my husband's breakfast, then bundled up and trudged out into the snow, slipping and sliding all the way to school. There I endangered life and limb, dodging hurtling teenage bodies in the halls as I searched for the designated teachers. I finally found both and hand-delivered the reports, then slowly slid my way toward home, stopping at the cleaners to leave my husband's suit and at the drugstore to get medicine for the sickening son.

Once home, I hurriedly straightened the house, made the beds, put out the mail, fed the cat, answered two phone calls, and fixed a hearty breakfast for the impatient patient. Finally, I was ready to leave for my meeting. As my son drowsily roused himself to inhale the breakfast, he noticed that it was now 9:35. He said, "I thought you were going to leave at 9:30. . . . Why are you ALWAYS LATE?"

What should I do, God? Should I get mad — or even? Should I run away from home or just put castor oil in his cough medicine?

Florence Nightingale

Dear Florence,

Children — or husbands — with bad colds are bad medicine for mothers. They can be hazardous to your mental health.

Just remember that a cold can't last more than a few days, so try to survive it as best you can. And for goodness sake, try not to catch the cold, because if YOU get sick, NO ONE will bother to bring you meals or medicine — much less, sympathy.

Think back to when your son was a toddler and you would be so worried when he had a cold. You would be careful to see that he took his medicine on time, and then you would rock him and read him stories and coax him to "eat just a little something for Mommy." Maybe your son remembers those days too. Maybe he's so demanding now because he's too old to be babied but still young enough to miss it.

So be patient, be brave, be careful not to catch the cold; and, if things get too bad, take two aspirin and call me in the morning.

God

Dear God,

Today I feel just like a plate-glass window. If anybody nudges me just a little bit, I will break all to pieces.

I know that's what happens to plate-glass windows because one time I nudged one — with my Volkswagen. Remember that, God?

My son was about four years old, and I had just bought a beat-up, second-hand Volkswagen. I wasn't quite used to driving it yet, so I was VERY careful when I drove down to the license office to get the new license plates.

I was only going about five miles an hour as I drove up to the curb to park. There was a handy parking spot near the license office, in front of an insurance company. I pulled slowly in and put on the brake, but the bug kept rolling. As I pushed on the brake harder and harder, it rolled slowly over the curb, across the sidewalk, and ever-so-gently nudged the plate-glass window.

Too late I realized that I had been stomping on the clutch instead of the brake, and I frantically applied the brake just as the plate-glass window came crashing down around us.

The man from the insurance office came up to me and said, "Lady, this is not a drive-in office. If you were in such a hurry, you could have just tooted your horn and I would have come out." He thought that was very funny. I did not.

My four-year-old son thought it was the most exciting thing that had ever happened to us. The minute we got home, he bolted from the car and began to broadcast the news of the happening to every neighbor in a six-block radius. I have never forgiven him for that.

But as usual, God, that was a long story to get to the point. Today I cannot take one more nudge — or I will self-destruct. I have been nudged once too often — by my family, neighbors, friends, and total strangers. I have been called on the phone and nudged to buy siding, storm windows, and lawn treatments. I have been nudged to serve on committees, bake cookies, work in the school cafeteria, help with a House Tour, and collect money door-to-door for a good cause. I'm beginning to think I have good cause to begrudge all these nudges.

I'm going to prop up my feet and close my eyes — and no matter who nudges, I'm not budging.

Breaking Point

Dear Breaking Point,

I think that's an inspired idea. You have a God-given right to take some of your own time for yourself. I know because I gave it to you.

It's good to be dedicated, dutiful, and dependable. It's noble to be involved and interested in causes and "into" every activity at church, school, and home. But enough nudging is enough.

You need time to rest and rekindle your fire . . . to remember the way things were and plan the way things will be or could be or should be. So while your eyes are closed, look inside. You haven't done that in a long time. Look to see who you are . . . what you are

. . . what you want to be. I don't think you're like a plate-glass window at all — easy to see through, easy to break. I think you're like a stained-glass window — full of beauty and color, dreams and visions — just waiting for my light to shine through and bring them to life. Breaking Point, I love you.

God

Dear God,

Keep this under your hat — I love hats.

Every time I see a display of hats I just have to stop and try some on — and I almost always find one that I want to take home with me. There's only one problem, God. That's just about the only place I can take the hat — home. Nobody wears hats anymore, so if I get up enough courage to wear one somewhere, I stick out like a dandelion on the White House lawn or a hot-fudge sundae at a Weight Watchers' banquet.

In my closet — on the top shelf, back in the dark where no one can see — I have hats made of black straw, red straw, brown felt, green felt, and yellow felt. I have a floppy straw hat like you could wear on a picnic (if you were Scarlett O'Hara) and a medium-sized straw hat just right for gardening and a smaller straw hat for driving. I have a fat fur hat for very cold, a knitted hat for regular cold, and a little cap for just cool. You can see that I have let hats go to my head.

Every once in a while, I even get real brave and wear one of my hats. Wearing a hat makes me feel glamorous, special, "all together," sophisticated — and out of place.

What should I do, God? Should I go on being a Mad Hatter, or should I give up and give them away so they can go to somebody else's head?

Bee in My Bonnet

Dear Bee in Your Bonnet,

We all have our little problems — and yours is certainly a *little* one. But I know what you mean. Should you go ahead and "be you" and risk looking different and maybe even a little ridiculous? Or should you squelch that little spark of difference and play it safe and blend into the crowd?

Well, Bee, I'm sorry to have to tell you that this is one question you'll have to answer for yourself. I can't do all your thinking for you — that's why I gave you a mind of your own.

If safety and security are important to you, then don't take the risk. Go ahead and blend into the crowd. There's nothing wrong with being "one of the gang," as long as the gang isn't breaking any laws — either mine or the state's.

But if you feel it's important to assert your individuality to save your spirit, your personality, your self-image — then take the risk and be YOU no matter who smirks or snickers.

I can't tell you which to do, but I must admit that it always gives me a good laugh when you show up at church in one of those crazy hats of yours.

God

Dear God,

Did you know my brother-in-law is the most-photographed man in the world? I bet you thought it was Robert Redford or Prince Charles. No . . . no . . . it's my brother-in-law.

That's because he spends a lot of time with my sister, and you can't be with her more than ten minutes before she has taken your picture. If I didn't know better, I would think she was from Japan because she doesn't go ANYWHERE without a camera in her hand.

Since my sister and her husband travel a lot, she has so many pictures that she could do a travelogue at the drop of a light switch. There you would see my brother-in-law next to the Parthenon in Greece, in front of the Eiffel Tower in France, shaking hands with a bullfighter or a bull in Spain, leaning against the leaning tower, kissing the Blarney Stone, and buying another roll of film for my sister at Disneyland.

Actually, it's a wonderful hobby. Her grandchildren will inherit a pictorial history of our family AND of the world. If they want to, they can spend every winter evening for the rest of their lives looking through family albums.

On the other hand, MY grandchildren — if I ever have any — will have to spend winter evenings twiddling their thumbs. All they will inherit is some snapshots of our wedding (we didn't even hire a photographer because we thought informal shots would be more fun, so another brother-in-law shot us with his candid camera) and a camera with a roll of film in it from 1976 that I never did remember to get developed. What should I do, God? Do you think my future grandchildren will feel culturally deprived?

Out of the Picture

Dear Out of the Picture,

It's lucky that you and your sister have the same family — now all you have to do is borrow your sister's negatives, have prints made, paste up a family album of your own, and maybe your grandchildren will never know the difference.

But the most important thing you can give them is memories — "thought pictures" of the times you spent together. Children seldom remember that you spent hours picking out just the right wallpaper for the dining room or that the garage was always in perfect order or the patio was swept clean at all times. They DO remember the picnics and the stories you read to them, the fun times on family vacations, the impromptu parties you had for their friends, the spur-of-the-moment late-night dash to get ice cream cones just before the ice cream store closes, Sunday dinners, and (I hope) Sunday mornings in church.

If you want to give your children and grandchildren a truly valuable gift, try to make going to church together a family tradition and a good memory. I want children to think of my house as a happy place so they will want to keep on visiting there after they grow up! Plan ahead so you won't have to argue or coax or cajole as you get ready to leave for church.

Maybe even plan a mini-celebration for afterward — a pancake breakfast at a restaurant or homemade sweet rolls or biscuits or something a little special at home. Use this time together to discuss the Scripture reading of the day or the lesson learned. Share thoughts and feelings about this visit to my house.

If you can pass on to the next generation a love for God and a commitment to church, family traditions, and happy memories, then a family album will be nice — but they won't ever need it to remember you.

God

Dear God,

Are you sure you hit the right button on the computer when you programmed "motivation" in children?

When my son was a toddler, he just LOVED to help Mommy and Daddy. He wanted to wash dishes, dust, cut the grass, empty the trash, repair the car, paint the house, build a doghouse — whatever we started to do, he was right there to volunteer his help.

Of course, his "helping" meant it would only take you about twice as long to get the job done — while you waited for him, showed him what to do, praised him, and carefully tried to keep him from noticing that you were secretly redoing everything he had done wrong.

But we assured ourselves it was worth it. This was good training — this would teach him how to REALLY help us when he got old enough.

Then, suddenly, he was a teenager. He was old enough, smart enough, tall enough to help. Now he could actually clear the table, do the dishes, cut the grass, take out the trash, and maybe even repair the car or paint the house.

There was only one thing wrong, God. You had only programmed his motivation to last until the day BEFORE he was old enough, smart enough, and tall enough.

Now what am I supposed to do, God? I managed to live through those toddlin' times, just waiting for the day when I would actually get some help around the house. Now the time has come, but the chore list is still hanging on the refrigerator door and there's not a single check on it to indicate that a single chore has been done. Not only that, God, but he isn't even home long enough for me to get rid of my frustration by fussing at him about it.

You managed to program enough motivation for him to want to get "involved" with things like school activities, a part-time job, dates, softball games with friends, movies, weekend trips, and even saving the whales or saving the world. But saving his parents? That motivation is definitely not in his program.

He will do no chore before its time — or during its time — or after its time. He has failed Basic Chore Skills. To him, a chore is a bore.

Based on this lack of Chore Motivation, he has developed the typical teen philosophy — keep a low profile, stay out of shouting range, and leave a chore undone long enough and your mother will finally get desperate enough to do it herself.

Where did we go wrong, God? How can we get our teen reprogrammed?

Hopeless

Dear Hopeless,

You are not alone. Most parents ask me why I made teenagers the way I did (and sometimes I wonder myself!).

You'll just have to accept the teen mentality as one of life's little mysteries. Be brave. Keep a stiff upper lip and a firm resolve. Try to maintain an open mind and open lines of communication . . . while you try to enforce your rules, your orders, and your authority.

Read all the articles you see about Teen Motivation — and then forget them. The only sure survival technique is prayer.

Come to think of it, maybe that's why I programmed teens the way I did — so I would hear from parents more often. So keep praying and keep hoping. And try not to just see the negative things about teenagers. This is a very special, beautiful, growing time of the spirit and the intellect and the personality. Look more closely. See the positive things. Enjoy them and rejoice in them. Actually, you have a wonderful son — even if he is poorly motivated at the moment.

God

Dear God,

I'm scared. I'm afraid I am becoming an endangered species.

I still believe in the Ten Commandments. I still believe in leading a moral life and going to church every Sunday. I even believe in Mom, apple pie, and the American flag.

But God, when I look around at the world, it seems like all those things are going out of style.

I've never been very good about being in style. I had long skirts when everybody else was wearing minis. And just when I finally got all my skirts short enough, long ones were back. I didn't learn to make quiche until the novelty had worn off and everybody was tired of eating it. I finally got a cute little Volkswagen just when it was no longer "in" to have one, so I looked cheap instead of avant-garde.

But it doesn't make any difference when those kinds of things go out of style, God. The scary thing is that it looks like a lot of people think YOU are out of style.

Every time I pick up a magazine or newspaper, it's quoting

statistics about how MANY young people believe in premarital sex or how FEW people think it's necessary to go to church anymore. And when Hollywood producers manage to make a good movie, they add some sort of scene or element that will make it a bit more "objectionable" so it will get a WORSE rating — because people don't want to be seen going to a "G" movie anymore unless they are under the age of ten or accompanied by a child! There was a time when no one would want to see any kind of movie EXCEPT a "G" rated one. What happened, God?

Are things as bad as they seem to me — or am I behind time again? Since I don't usually get in tune with a trend until it's almost over, is this one almost over, God? Are people starting to turn back to you? Am I still endangered, or are you coming back in style?

Scared

Dear Scared,

You probably didn't notice, but a few years ago people were asking "Is God dead?" They aren't asking that anymore, but now it seems that a lot of people think I'm on vacation — and they are going to get by with as much as they can before I get back in town!

But I DO think the tide is turning. Young people are beginning to "identify" with me, and people of all ages are starting to study and observe my commandments again. In fact, many people of today are beginning to see the commandments as I truly meant them. They listen to the negative command — "thou shalt not" — but they are also concerned with the positive law of love — "thou SHALT." As they obey my rules, they also spread my Good News. They help . . . they work . . . they care.

So don't be scared, Scared. My rating might not be as high as some of today's soap operas, but my fans still tune in regularly — and I'm getting new ones every day.

God

Dear God,

I have this terrible problem — right in my front yard. Recently, my mailbox has become a lot like Sodom and Gomorrah — or maybe a box of chocolate candy.

My mailbox is full of temptation. Every day I open it slowly and peek inside — and there they are — luring me on, leading me to the path of iniquity. It's those bright, shiny catalogs, God. Each one is full of pages with pictures of wonderful things I don't need but just HAVE to have! And they're just like candy — I can't ever stop with one. Once I choose one thing, I can't stop there. I have to have more and more.

Oh, there's no doubt about it, God. I have fallen under the influence of catalogs.

Just yesterday I approached my mailbox with caution — but there inside were six catalogs. I should have thrown them right in the wastebasket, but I just couldn't resist turning one page, and soon I was thumbing through them all. Before I realized it, I was making out order forms, writing out checks, and licking stamps for the envelopes. Once again, I had fallen.

And do you know what I ordered, God? Well, first there was a red flannel nightcap to wear while sleeping. It looked so cute in the picture and sounded so practical. The ad said you lose so-o-o much body heat through the top of your head; but if you wear this cap, you will always sleep toasty-warm. This means from now on I will always be a hot-head — and I'm afraid my husband will be too, once he sees me coming to bed in a red flannel cap!

Next I bought some cute little dishes to hold corn-on-the-cob. I really don't think this will change our lives for the better, but at the moment I thought for sure they were something I couldn't live without. Then there were some folding sunglasses (!), a clay butter-keeper, and a tie with a pattern of tiny anchors and the words "Don't give up the ship" for my son (because, at the moment, our son is threatening to change our lives for the better by joining the Navy).

But I really should have given up the ship — or the catalog — before I ordered the last thing. It is a genuine wooden, handmade bird-caller. I can just picture myself sitting on the patio, twirling it around, and driving all the birds in the neighborhood crazy when they come flying in to discover the biggest bird they have ever seen!

As you can see, God, things are desperate. I have catalog fever. Where will it all end? Should I chain up my mailbox — or my checkbook?

Do you think maybe the nightcap, folding sunglasses, corn dishes, and bird call really WILL change my life? Or do you think I should join Catalogs Anonymous?

Tempted

Dear Tempted,

Well, I hate to see you yielding to temptation, but I must admit I can't wait to see you wearing a red flannel nightcap and folding sunglasses while calling birds and feeding them on special corn dishes.

But seriously, you do seem to have a problem. Why don't you go through the next batch of catalogs and check all the things you think you want — but instead of ordering them, just put the catalogs away for about two weeks? THEN look at your selections again and see if you still can't live without them. Total the costs to see if all those little things won't add up to a bigger amount than you suspected — an amount you might use to buy one valuable thing or some special treat for the family. (Though it's hard to imagine a more special treat for the family than seeing you in that nightcap!)

And then maybe you could try this in other areas of your life also. When you are tempted to say something critical of someone, put it away for a little while and see if you STILL want to say that. When you are tempted to lose your temper, remove yourself from the situation for a minute — step into the garage or go out in the yard (just don't go near the mailbox!) — and see if you really can't live without sharing your bad temper with others. Sometimes you HAVE to shout or stomp just to get someone's attention (like a teenager's), but usually you can lay down the law without raising your voice or lowering your dignity.

So, Tempted, the only thing you really need to order is patience, fortitude, and good judgment. They're only available from MY catalog, and some people think they cost too much. But, once you get them, it will be a lot easier to find the Bluebird of Happiness — even without a genuine handmade bird-caller.

God

Dear God,

I have just realized that the American way of life is a lot like iced tea. Do you think we should try to change that?

Just think about iced tea. We use boiling water to make it hot . . . then add ice cubes to make it cold . . . next we stir in sugar to make it sweet, and finally add lemon juice to make it sour. It's the same with lots of things we do.

We put all kinds of fertilizer on our lawns to make the grass grow, then spend most of the summer cutting and trimming it. We break our backs applying some miracle ingredient that will remove the ugly wax buildup on our kitchen floors, and then immediately put on a fresh coat of wax so it can start building up again. We take cooking classes and study cookbooks so we can become gourmet cooks, and as soon as we learn what to do in the kitchen we quit doing it and eat only lettuce and yogurt so we can lose weight.

When it comes to clothing, we expect men (who usually complain that they are too hot) to wear heavy, three-piece suits to the same party where women (who usually complain that they are too cold) are expected to wear flimsy, silky party dresses.

We spend endless hours teaching our children to walk and talk, and as soon as they learn, we tell them to sit down and shut up.

Well, God, maybe I shouldn't use the word "we" so freely. Surely everyone doesn't operate this way, but it DOES seem to be the typical American life-style — full of contradictions and frustrations.

Did we miss something somewhere, God? Someone once said that life is the original do-it-yourself project. Did we read the directions wrong?

Concerned

Dear Concerned,

Yes, life IS a do-it-yourself project all right — but the directions are a little different for each person. So try not to be too concerned with the contradictions and frustrations. Change the things you can . . . accept the things you can't . . . and pray for wisdom to know the difference. (Someone else said that a long time ago, and it's STILL an excellent do-it-yourself direction to remember.)

And, when you're in the middle of the grass cutting and the floor waxing and the tea icing, here's something else to remember: The songwriter Irving Berlin said, "Life is ten percent what you make it and ninety percent how you take it."

God

Dear God,

Help! I'm being swept under by a paper avalanche! I am knee-deep in newspapers, mired down in magazines, and lost in a sea of letters.

I love to read and I want to read it all — but if this is a Paper Chase, I'm losing. I have never been known for speed (in reading or anything else), and I need to be the champion speed-reader of all time just to get through each day's accumulation.

The morning and evening newspapers keep piling up, and I can't bear to throw them away until I've gone through them. Who knows what morsel of news, tidbit of trivia, or glimmer of gossip I might miss? I might even learn something!

And then there are the magazines. They're all so glossy with such beautiful pictures and articles with intriguing titles like: "Dial a Shrink" — "The Slang Gap" — "Year of the Cucumber" — "An Archaeologist's Deepest Digs." Who could throw away articles like that before they've been read?

And the letters. We seldom get letters from anybody we know, but we DO get lots of letters from insurance companies, loan companies, carpet cleaners, automobile dealers, specialty shops, and, of course, more magazines and newspapers asking us to subscribe. I find it fairly easy to throw away the letters, but I still take time to at least glance through them to be sure I'm not missing anything.

I have stacked newspapers in the garage and in the basement. I have hidden magazines beside the couch and under the dresser. And I have thrown out so many letters the garbage man is getting a stiff back. But every day, more paper comes into the house than I can read through and throw out.

I am saving my money to try to get enough to take one of those expensive speed-reading courses, but I am so busy shuffling papers that I don't know how I can shuffle my schedule enough to find time to get to the classes.

I'm being papered into a corner, God. How can I escape?

Paper Plagued

Dear Paper Plagued,

You are living in a time when MORE is being written about LESS than ever before! So be selective. It's important to keep informed, so you should glance through the newspapers and magazines and letters and maybe even invest in the speed-reading course. But once the paper explosion has gotten out of hand, the best thing for you to do is to package it all and give it to the nearest Boy Scout. He'll be the hero of the next paper drive.

But when you talk about all that paper piling up at your house, you don't mention a word about any kind of RELIGIOUS reading material. Have you thought about reading a good religious book or newspaper or magazine? I hope you'll find time for that.

And, Paper Plagued, after you've given the Boy Scout all those leftovers, there's something you can read that will give you more good news than any newspaper, more helpful ideas than any magazine, and more inspiration than any book. It's called the Bible. I highly recommend it.

God

Dear God,

Did you know that in 1833 the head of the U.S. Patent Office resigned because he thought everything of significance had already been invented? And then, of course, along came the automobile, the telephone, the airplane, television, microwave ovens, video recorders, computers, and a few little things like that.

I know just how that man must have felt. I am always looking around this house and thinking I should resign because everything of significance has already been done. We've gotten the carpets cleaned, the walls washed, the house painted, the bricks tuck-pointed, the insulation added, the drapes cleaned and put back up, the oven scoured, and the refrigerator cleaned out. What else could there possibly ever be to be done?

Then the next day a big crack appears in the driveway and needs to be repaired; the people next door call to say they have had their house treated for termites so the termites may be headed our way and we should have our house checked immediately; two storm windows mysteriously crack and should be replaced; the latch on the gate quits working and the wind starts banging it so we should fix it quick before the hinges break; the gas grill stops working; and the garden hose springs a leak.

Is this any way to live — from one "significant" event to the next? Must a homeowner man the crisis hotline from sun to sun? Is a homeowner's work never done?

I put up a sign that says "God Bless Our Home" — maybe I should put up a second one that says "God Bless Our Home Repairs." How much longer can this go on, God? When can I resign?

Tired of It All

Dear Tired of It All,

Instead of resigning, you should become resigned to the fact that "Home is where the heartburn is." The price you have to pay for enjoying the comforts of home is taking care of all the uncomfortable maintenance jobs.

But the jobs you've mentioned are only HOUSE maintenance. Your main job is HOME maintenance — filling it with love and laughter and prayer.

So be grateful you have a lovely house, and do whatever you can to keep it in good repair — but always remember the most "significant" thing you can do is to put your house in order so it will always be "home sweet home."

God

Dear God,

On a television program this morning I heard someone describe a woman this way: "She looked like a classic statue that had been put out in the weather." That's exactly how I feel today, God.

Well, actually, I'm not all that classic, but I sure am weathered. My skin feels like it's spent a week in the Sahara. My hair looks like it's been in one windstorm too many. And my bones feel like I've been walking against the wind five miles too far.

What do you do on a day like this, God? Do you jump back in bed and pull the covers over your head and wait for sundown? Do you drive to a strange city where you won't run into anyone you know so you can get the grocery shopping done? Do you grab your piggy bank and dash to the nearest beauty salon that offers emergency repair service? Or do you just sit in a corner, rocking back and forth, alternately eating chocolate candy bars and sucking your thumb?

Quick, God, this signal is not a test. This is the real thing — a crisis alert. I need intensive care.

Weatherbeaten

Dear Weatherbeaten,

Remember — beauty is only skin deep — and I know this is the kind of day that you'd like to solve things by jumping out of your skin. But since you can't do that, all the ideas you had sound good to me. Take a drive, go to a beauty salon, or sit in the corner. OR — you could do something constructive. Forget about your own feelings by giving your day to someone else.

Stay home and write all the overdue letters you owe or call and chat with someone you know is lonely. Or take that drive, but to a nursing home or hospital. When you see the big problems there, it might be easier to forget your little ones.

And, if none of these things work and you still feel weatherbeaten, just put a sack over your head and tell your family that you are today's Mystery Mother.

God

Dear God,

Today my son explained to me that he was born with a special lens in his eye. It's like a contact lens except his is a NON-contact lens. Instead of helping him to see better, this lens KEEPS him from seeing one thing — dirt. Because of this lens, he can't see dirty clothes on the floor, dirty glasses by his chair, dirty plates under his bed, or dirty fingerprints on the ceiling.

What should I do, God? How can I keep from laughing when he springs his tall stories on me like that? How can I still look stern and spout orders? How can I think up a better story to top his?

It's not easy living with an imaginative child in the house, God. You have to always be on your toes, ready for the next alibi, the next adventure or project, the next flight of fancy.

Should I let him get by with this latest and pick up after him? Or should I rub his nose in it?

Torn

Dear Torn,

Always delight in creativity — and in children. All too soon the children are grown and gone. All too soon they forfeit imagination in order to face the realities of maturity.

Sometimes you make too much of a little dirt and a little clutter; so, in a way, it's wonderful that your son can be happily oblivious to it. It would also be wonderful if he could pass through the world without seeing the dirt there — and without being touched by it.

There's only one problem — although he doesn't see the dirt, it's still there. And, unfortunately, he and his generation overlook too much of the dirt in today's world so it never gets cleaned up.

So it's YOUR responsibility to wipe the smile off your face long enough to point out to your son HIS responsibility.

Love the sinner, but don't excuse the sin.

God

Dear God,

I have this terrible problem. I would like to be rich for a day — or a week — or a while. I don't have to be REAL rich, but I would just like to know how it feels to buy something because I like it instead of because I like the price tag.

God, I am sick of being second-hand Hannah. Half the things I own are second-hand treasures from garage sales. I drive a second-hand car. I live in a second-hand house and have a second-hand typewriter. We even had a second-hand dog — a "previously owned" canine from the Humane Society. And now we have a second-hand cat — it actually belongs to a neighbor but has decided to adopt us as a second-hand family.

I want to have something first-hand. I want to have something that's priceless — because I don't NEED TO KNOW the price!

I have this crazy desire to go shopping at a fancy dress shop and not have to feel embarrassed because the sales lady is obviously richer than I am. I want to go to an elegant French restaurant and order a meal without looking at the right side of the menu for the prices first. I want to fly down to Acapulco or take a cruise on the *Love Boat* or just go out of town ANYWHERE for a weekend — without worrying about how much it costs. I would even like to go out for lunch with the girls and be able to say "I'll pick up the tab today," so we don't have to go through that bit of dividing it by seven and then deducting the salad Jane didn't get and adding on for the dessert Sally had and trying to decide if the Bleu Cheese dressing was extra.

Forgive me for complaining, God, but remember you said, "Blessed are the lowly for they shall inherit the earth"? When, God, when?

Lowly

Dear Lowly,

I guess I don't need to tell you how rich you already are — in family, friends, and faith. You know that already. You don't want to hear that. You want to hear about money and material possessions.

Well, Lowly, if you inherited the earth, you would inherit a lot of people poorer than you are, people who would LIKE to have even second-hand belongings. But you don't want to hear that either. Maybe I should tell you that rich people aren't always happy people — but I know you'd like to have the chance to find out for yourself.

So all I can tell you, Lowly, is to save your money. Instead of buying all those garage sale things, save up and buy one "something" so expensive that the sales lady can't possibly look down her nose at you. Instead of going out for pizza or hamburgers so often, save up and treat yourself to that French restaurant meal. And be sure and enter all the sweepstakes and maybe you'll get lucky and win a trip on the *Love Boat*.

Sorry, Lowly, I know you don't think this is a very good answer, but just remember that half the fun of life is wishing and hoping —

and you're really good at both. So enjoy what you have — don't waste it waiting for something better to come along.

And I'll tell you a secret. Do you know that sometimes those expensive French restaurants actually serve snails and octopus? Wouldn't you really rather have a good hamburger with lots of onions? And have you ever thought about the fact that almost EVERYTHING in Buckingham Palace is second-hand? See — you're not as lowly as you thought!

God

Dear God,

Did you know that in Winchester, Massachusetts, it's against the law for a young girl to be employed to dance on a tightrope — except in church? In Maine it's against the law to whistle on Sunday, and an Alabama law says that anyone who wears a false mustache in church and causes unseemly laughter is liable to arrest!

Did you know about these "church laws," God?

I don't have much luck laying down the law at my house, and that's why I decided to read this "law" book yesterday and discovered all those strange old laws that once were binding — and some of them are even worse than the laws at my house.

In Connecticut, it's against the law to sell pickles which collapse when dropped twelve inches — the pickles should remain whole and even bounce! At my house, it's against the law to bounce pickles or bounce loud rock music off the wall when Mommy or Daddy has had a bad day.

We don't have any laws about tightrope walking or whistling or wearing a false mustache, but we DO forbid shooting paperclips across the room with a rubber band, aiming for the photograph of Great Grandma Davids. We have passed an ordinance prohibiting the neighbor's cat from walking all over our car, leaving dusty footprints, and the neighbor's dog from racing across the street, barking and growling at us as though we were Public Enemy Number One every time we step onto our own front porch.

We have a law against leaving muddy boots dripping INSIDE the house and school books dripping OUTSIDE the house in the rain. We have laws about dribbling cheese from a pizza into the shag carpet or shaking a Coke bottle to see if it will erupt like Mount St. Helens in the kitchen.

Oh yes, God, we have lots of laws. But here's our problem — how do we go from laws to law enforcement?

Not Supercop

Dear Not Supercop,

Maybe you've asked the wrong person. I only made ten laws — and it isn't easy to enforce them either.

Your laws all sound reasonable and enforceable to me — but then I thought mine were, too.

Of course, you have to have love to balance law. So if you spread enough of that around, maybe a little cheese on the carpet and some bouncing pickles will just make your house a home.

And there's one consolation — at least your laws and my laws are easier to enforce than the one in Brawley, California, where a resolution was passed forbidding SNOW within the city limits!

God

Dear God,

I have this crumby problem — because my husband has a crumby habit. I could serve that man only a toothpick and a glass of water, and when he got up from the table there would be crumbs all over the tabletop, on the floor, on the chair — crumbs, crumbs everywhere.

When my son was about two years old he could do a pretty good job of redecorating the walls with oatmeal designs and filling his shoes with pureed spinach, but even he could not manufacture crumbs the way my husband can.

My better half attacks a piece of toast like it is a plague of locusts that he can wipe out with his butter knife. He takes a tiny dab of butter and smears it back and forth, faster and faster — crumbs flying everywhere — until the butter is battered, the toast is tattered, and he has beaten his breakfast into submission. He takes the same approach to lunch, dinner, and anyone who differs with his views of the American way of life.

What should I do, God? How can I keep my kitchen crumb-free without damaging my husband's psyche? Should I sit quietly by while he takes out his hostility on hot buttered biscuits and defenseless muffins? Should I be subtle and sweep him off his feet by sweeping around his chair in the middle of every meal? Or should I just come flat out with it and tell my husband he's crumby?

Clean Sweep

Dear Clean Sweep,

I've noticed those crumbs flying around your table — and I know that must be very irritating, spending the best years of your life as a crumb-catcher. But everyone has little bad habits, and at least your husband's habit isn't illegal, immoral, or fattening. So just overlook his crumbiness and take out some of your own hostility when you are cleaning up after him.

And by the way, Clean Sweep, did you realize that you have a little mealtime habit of your own? Just when you get comfortably settled, with your plate piled high before you, you kick off your shoes under the table. Sometimes a shoe lands under your husband's foot. Sometimes he stumbles over a shoe when he gets up to get dessert. Sometimes you even pad off barefoot, leaving the shoes under the table until the next day. This COULD be very irritating to others. It could be enough to make a man tackle his toast. (At least that's what your husband told me yesterday!)

God

Dear God,

My son is always asking me embarrassing questions such as "Why?" "Who says so?" "Are you SURE?" That last one always throws me off-balance. I immediately feel insecure and NOT sure.

But the worst is when I use a popular expression and he says: "What is that supposed to mean?" I never know.

I say "by George" or "for Pete's sake," and he wants to know who George and Pete are. I say "I'm hot as a firecracker," and he reminds me that a firecracker is only hot when it explodes. That usually makes me explode.

Today I foolishly said "I'm as happy as a clam" and was immediately unhappy that I had said it. On the surface, it would appear that a clam's life-style is not to be desired. Clams never go to Hollywood parties or get asked to appear on talk shows. They don't seem to have much of a family life, and I never see clams on vacation unless they're next to a piece of parsley on my plate.

And what about "tired as a dog"? How tired can a dog be when all he does all day is eat and sleep? Or "mad as an old wet hen." How can you tell when a chicken is angry — wet or dry? Where did all these expressions come from, God?

Maybe my son is right — maybe I should watch my language!

Cliché Prone

Dear Cliché Prone,

Yes, maybe you SHOULD be a little more careful when you speak — especially to that smart-aleck son of yours. Maybe you'd better tell him to speak to you more carefully, too!

But he DOES have a valid complaint about those expressions. They sure sound silly today, but actually many of them have interesting meanings — if they're used correctly!

For example, "happy as a clam" is only HALF the proper expression. Since clams bury themselves in mud or sand, the only time the clam digger can find them is when the tide is out — so the original saying was "I'm happy as a clam at high tide!" Now that makes sense.

So be careful when you use an expression — or tell a story — to be sure you tell it right. Don't forget the punch line.

Be especially careful when you're talking about religion. Don't tell your son half-truths. If you don't really know the answer, look it up.

It's so easy for children to misunderstand the messages you are giving them if you are lazy about using the right words or expressions. You might jokingly say, "God will get you for that" and a child might remember that and think of me as a scarey "bogey man" instead of a loving father.

So, Cliché Prone, be careful to give your son the WHOLE truth about your faith and what you believe — and don't be afraid to talk to him about me. If parents are embarrassed to talk about religion and the things they hold dear and the values they live by, the next generation won't realize how important it is to cherish my teachings and my truths — and they'll never get to know me as you do.

But before we get off the subject of clams, do you know what the poet Ogden Nash said about them? He said,

"When you're lolling on a piazza,

It's what you are as happy as a."

So, Cliché Prone, go on being happy as a clam and pass this on to the next generation, too!

God

Dear God,

I am depressed. I have been watching and listening to commercials again.

Now, here I sit, waiting for brown "age" spots to show up on my hands; blue circles to appear under my eyes; wrinkles to pop out all over my body; and stress symptoms to give me a headache and an upset stomach.

I feel a cold coming on, and my throat is getting itchy; my arches are falling, and my blood pressure is rising; my muscles are getting stiff, and my hairdo is getting limp.

What should I do, God? Every time I see a problem described, I'm sure I've got it or am going to get it any minute now. I'm worried about adolescent pimples, even though it's been so long since I was an adolescent that I can't even remember it anymore. I am worried about getting stranded in a strange city after losing my travelers' checks, even though I can't get to any strange cities because I have developed a fear of flying, driving, bicycling, and walking — after watching the six o'clock news. And besides, I don't have an American Express card — and I can't leave home without it!

Depressed

Dear Depressed,

You certainly are "suggestible." Now if you could just convert that to something POSITIVE — like when your husband suggests that you should stop being late all the time!

The next time you start to feel your sinuses clogging and your stomach churning, take a walk and drink in the beauty around you — it's good medicine and the best drink in the world. Then take some of the positive suggestions in those commercials. Care enough to send the very best — and send yourself to visit someone who really is sick or someone who lives alone and is sick of it.

Or reach out and touch someone — maybe someone in your own family — who might be in desperate need of a hug or an affirmative word. Call someone you think might profit from a phone visit. Or come visit me. I'll tell you about some positive suggestions I put in a commercial one time.

They're known as the "Beatitudes" and they go something like this:

Blessed are those who hunger and thirst for holiness. . . .

Blessed are the persecuted . . . the single-hearted . . . the peacemakers. . . .

Blessed are they who show mercy. . . .

Take a minute now to look up the Beatitudes in the Bible and write them down on a little card — then don't leave home without it!

God

Dear God,

I would love to sit around a campfire and earn merit badges by making things out of popsicle sticks and maybe even become an "Eagle" — but I'll never be able to join the Boy Scouts. "Be Prepared" could never be my motto.

Nothing in my background, schooling, or innermost psyche has prepared me for the things that happen at my house.

Just yesterday my son came in and said: "Prepare to be a percussion instrument." I was not prepared.

Somehow I could not come up with an idea of what the prerequisites were for percussion!

To my son, it was simple. He happened to have two pencils in his hand and — suddenly — he had been hit by the urge to use these pencils as drumsticks. And — since I was the nearest object at the moment, I was chosen to be the drum, the "percussion instrument" for his fanfare.

So, while I was still in my daze of indecision, he proceeded to drum on my arm, knee, shoulder, etc. — parump, parumping — while launching into the tale of some exciting happening at school. Unprepared as I was, I found that being a percussion instrument can be fun, and soon we were giggling and chortling about his school news flash of the day and the accompanying drum fanfare.

But you see what I mean, God? Tomorrow it will probably happen again. Someone in the family or a friend or a neighbor — or even a total stranger who knocks on the door — will surprise me with a new idea or project or challenge. And I won't be prepared!

Did I miss something somewhere? Was there a course I should have taken or a book I should have read? Why do I always seem to be unprepared for the daze of my life?

Not a Boy Scout

Dear Not a Boy Scout,

Don't sign up for night school or try to soar with the "Eagles." Of course, there are SOME things you should try to prepare for — but not ALL of life.

If you plan to be a nuclear scientist, you shouldn't just hope the formulas will come to you in a dream and you'll get a big bang out of it. If you plan to be a homemaker, you can't just hope you'll be able to rub two eggs together and get a French omelette. You have to study and work for what you want.

But nothing will prepare you for all the surprises of life — because I prepared it that way! Now you will never get bored. Your days will be filled with excitement . . . mystery . . . suspense . . . and fun!

I know. Sometimes the surprises seem to be bad or sad. Sometimes they mean sacrifice or hard work or grief and tears. But trust me. There's a reason for the not-so-good ones too.

And sometimes all you need is the vision and the faith to see the surprises as opportunities. Then, prepared or not, you can enjoy life — even on those days when you are beat upon so much you feel like a percussion instrument!

God

Dear God,

I have this terrible problem. My family won't let me be sick!

Anybody else at my house can get sick and stay in bed while I dash in with pills and potions, hot lunches and cold compresses, and a generous dose of tender loving care.

But when I get sick, my family dashes in with dirty laundry and empty dishes, whining: "I don't have any clean socks" — "Aren't we having dinner tonight?" — "Aren't you ever going to the store again — we are out of EVERYTHING!"

Oh, I can GET sick all right — with as many sniffles, coughs, aches, and mystery ailments as they have. It's just that they won't let me BE sick or STAY sick. If it took one of them two weeks to recover from some kind of flu, I am supposed to bounce back from the same flu in about twenty minutes.

It's OK if I take an aspirin and rest on the sofa for just a few minutes — but that's it! That should be enough of a miracle cure to heal any ailment — and I should be ready to jump up and get the house humming again.

What should I do about this, God? When I get sick, my family gets sickening! And I am sick of it.

Failing Fast

Dear Failing Fast,

Everybody has a right to be sick — or sickening — once in a while. So it looks like you are going to have to exert your rights and demand a little attention. And yet, if you think about it a minute, you'll see that it's nice to be so needed and so indispensable to a family. There are a lot of lonely people who would like to know that feeling.

Even *I* want to feel needed and indispensable. Yet today many people seem to think they don't need my help anymore and think they can handle everything by themselves. Fortunately, you are not one of those people, Failing Fast. You don't think you can handle ANYTHING without me. But I'm not complaining. I'm glad you come to me and put your hand in my hand. There is nothing you and I can't handle — together.

So the next time you start failing, just pull the covers up over your head and let the members of your family do their own cooking and laundry. And if they don't serve up enough tender loving care, call on me. Remember, I still make house calls.

God

Dear God,

Do you think the word YONKERS is just the name of a place in New York? Well, to my son it's an "expletive deleted."

He was going through that phase when he wanted to use "questionable" words to express his anger or frustration, and we were having quite a few "discussions" about his choice of words. Then one day when he was mad, he suddenly said YONKERS!

When I looked surprised, he explained that he had decided he could keep out of trouble and still get rid of his anger if he made up his own "expletive." He had chosen YONKERS.

After that, we started thinking of some other places that might make good expletives just because of the way the sounds roll off your tongue. We thought of BiLOXi, ScheNECtady, TallaHASSee, and a few others. But then I began wondering if this was such a good idea.

Does it matter what you say, God — or how you say it?

Word Watcher

Dear Word Watcher,

Well, that IS a good question. And the answer is — BOTH. Some people can say "God" and it's a curse. Others say "God" and it's a beautiful prayer.

It's always important to watch what you're saying — but also HOW you're saying it.

Today, many people use my name in vain and don't seem to think anything of it. I wish they wouldn't do that. Others give me great honor by speaking my name as a prayer or as the name of a friend.

I hope that's the way you and your family will always use my name, Word Watcher. But the next time you hit your thumb with the hammer, I won't be troubled if I hear you say YONKERS or KALAMAZOO or TIMBUCKTOO or even DEUTERONOMY.

God

Dear God,

I have decided that I can't run for President of the United States. You know why? Because of supper.

I don't know how those lady politicians do it — but I know I can't. If the hotline from Russia rang at my house, I'd have to tell the Russians to call back later because it was time for me to fix supper. If I was summoned to an emergency summit conference, I'd have to say I couldn't make it because I had to get home in time to take something out of the freezer for supper.

If I walked in my front door, clutching a trophy for having just set a record time in swimming the English Channel, no one would even notice my bathing suit was dripping on the carpet — they'd just want to know why supper was late.

I could work a twelve-hour day and drive thirty miles home on an ice-covered highway, and the minute I staggered through the door I would hear "How long till supper?"

Once I get supper ready, they probably won't like it anyway and somebody will say "Casserole again?" But for better or worse, they want SOMETHING on the table so they can either consume or complain.

What should I do, God? Should my whole life have to hinge on supper? Must I always be shopping for, cooking for, or cleaning up after supper? Is supper really destined to be my main contribution to life on this planet?

Suppered Out

Dear Suppered Out,

I always thought supper was a wonderful idea — the family gathered around the table, sharing food and ideas and happenings of the day, just like a Norman Rockwell painting. And if this could really happen at houses all over the world every night, it WOULD be a major contribution to life on your planet.

But I know families aren't always picture perfect, and with today's busy pace it must be frustrating to have to come up with something 365 times a year. And besides, I didn't mean for supper to be your ONLY contribution — so you do need help.

First, haven't you heard about TV dinners and "carry-out" food? I think maybe those lady politicians are well acquainted with these. Or what about time-sharing? Couldn't you teach someone in your family to cook so you could *share* supper cooking? (You'd be doing them a favor and yourself, too. They may learn to love it, and you'd have a backup in case you got a broken hand or had a nervous breakup or breakdown.)

Or why don't you use your "subtle" powers of persuasion to convince someone at your house to take up the "hobby" of French cooking or barbecuing or Chinese cookery or maybe even eating out at gourmet restaurants! Then you'd have a break occasionally.

But I think you might as well face the fact that most of the time you'll still be the one expected to get supper on the table. And it's not all bad — to be thought of as the provider of sustenance, the source of yummies for the tummy, the one who holds the secrets of the skillet and the saucepan. It's good to be the responsible Martha, but you have to find a way to be Mary too — so you can have time to sit at my feet and listen.

God

Dear God,

Why is it that everything at my house plays hide-and-seek when I'm in a hurry?

When it's a dark, dreary day with rain pouring down and I'm running late, I dash to the closet and grab one boot and put it on. Then I reach for the other one. It's never there. It's hiding.

I frantically feel around in the dark recesses of the closet, but no luck. Then I start hopping around the room, with one boot on and one boot off, looking under the bed, in the other closet, and anywhere else I can think of. Finally, in desperation, I go back to the first closet and search more frantically. There, peeking out from behind the edge of my raincoat is the other boot. It was there all the time — hiding.

When it's a bright, sunshiny day, I grab my purse and reach for my sunglasses. Are they on the shelf where they should be? Of course not. They're hiding. I look in my scarf drawer, my other purse, all my coat pockets, and the kitchen catch-all drawer. Finally I give up and jump in the car without them. As I take my car keys out of my purse, I look again. There, smugly winking up at me, are the hide-and-seeking sunglasses.

And my refrigerator is even worse! Just when I have supper all on the table, piping hot and ready to eat, I reach into the refrigerator for the one last thing I forgot. Whatever it is — catsup, tartar sauce, butter, jelly — it isn't there. While the food cools and my temper heats, I find wilted lettuce and leftover bologna, the last piece of chicken from last week's picnic, and the grated cheese I was looking for YESTERDAY to go on last night's spaghetti, but NEVER what I am looking for NOW. It's hiding — behind a milk carton, under a foil-wrapped mystery package, or between my son's refrigerated science experiment and my never-fail-recipe dessert that failed.

What should I do, God? Why do I have peek-a-boo possessions? Why can't I ever find my wool gloves, the telephone bill (that I THINK is due today), my reading glasses, the spare umbrella, or the button that goes on the blouse that I just HAVE to wear to the luncheon tomorrow?

Is my house haunted by a hide-and-seek specter or a peek-a-boo poltergeist? Must I spend every day on a search-and-rescue mission? Should I buy a bloodhound or hire a psychic or take private detective lessons? Things are getting desperate and I HAVE to do something. I would have written to you about this sooner, but I couldn't find the stamps.

Searching

Dear Searching,

It wouldn't take much searching to see that you should forget the hound, psychic, and detective lessons and take a MEMORY course. I might also suggest that you get your house better organized, but we both know that organization is one area where you are never going to be voted "most likely to succeed."

But don't worry, Searching, there are a lot of hide-and-seek houses like yours today. They're caused by too little time, too many involvements, and the absentmindedness that seems to be a symptom of the modern hectic life-style.

But you know, symptoms usually make you start looking for a cure — so you really should start working on the idea of "a place for everything and everything in its place." You might be surprised at how much time it would save — and then you would have some extra time to search for more important things.

You could search for new ways to "find" your family — to discover how to ease their burden or encourage a dream or bandage a hidden hurt. You could search for a book of hidden poetry to read just for the beauty of it (you haven't done that in a long time) or a new song that would make your heart sing. You could search for a new friend. (Old friends are best, but new friends often give you new insights and fresh viewpoints — and sometimes turn into old friends!) You could search for a new hobby, a new diet, a new exercise for physical fitness, or even a new dress (just be sure to hang it in the FRONT of the closet so you'll be able to find it).

And when you're through with all your earthly searching, come to me. Seek and you shall find, knock and it shall be opened unto you.

God

Dear God,

You must have had a lot of fun designing the teenaged mind — giving it 90% creativity, 1% neatness, 40% silliness, 40% super seriousness, 80% evasion, and 100% hunger. You say that's 351%? Well, teens are good at exaggeration, too. But with such a mixture, how do you ever expect parents to keep up with the teenagers?

I am always amazed at their creative approach to problem-solving. Last week I asked a teenaged friend what he thought we should do about the deteriorating upholstery in the back seat of our old Volkswagen. Immediately he had an answer: "Just fill the back seat with dirt and plant flowers there." Now why didn't I think of that?

A few days later, I told my teenaged son that I needed to buy some wedding presents, and asked if he had any suggestions about what I should buy. He thought for a minute and then came up with his idea of a perfect gift — a metal detector.

I have seen people using these contraptions in parks and places like that — holding the long handle with the detector on the end of it — looking for coins or other metal objects that might have been lost in the grass. But I would never have thought of a metal detector for a wedding gift.

I was too stunned to ask for an explanation. All I could think of was a lovely outdoor reception with lots of flowers, green grass, birds singing, all the guests dressed beautifully, sipping punch out of little cups, and the bride, in her flowing white dress and veil, moving slowly among the guests, using her metal detector!

His second choice for a wedding gift was a Fuzz Buster (one of those little things you put in your car to warn you when a policeman is in the area, checking your speed with radar). Maybe he thought that would come in handy for the honeymoon trip. Who knows?

Who knows ANYTHING about teens — except that their minds are tuned to a different channel. And if anyone ever doubts their creativity or ingenuity, just ask one of them why the car came home late or why the homework isn't finished. As soon as you hear the answer you will have no doubt that CREATIVITY LIVES!

With all this imagination you gave them, God, how are we parents ever going to compete? How will we ever think of good reasons for them to be home at 10 P.M. or cut the grass BEFORE they go to the movie or sit up straight, keep their hair combed, speak intelligently and intelligibly to our friends, and never question our unimaginative solutions to household problems? I hate to always have to answer "just BECAUSE. . . . "

What's a parent to do, God?

Wondering

Dear Wondering,

Parents don't have to "compete" with teens. All they have to do is believe in them, dream with them, and love them. And expect and demand the same in return. You won't always get it immediately, but you have to keep expecting it and demanding it. And because you ARE the parent, sometimes the answer "just BECAUSE . . . " should be enough.

But I am wondering, too, about those teens. I think I did a pretty good design job, and I am tired of hearing so many people complain about it.

The only stories people spread are the ones about the "bad" teens, the troublesome ones. There are a lot of good teens — terrific teens! And they're not just creative. They're interesting because of their fresh view of life. They're fun because of their spontaneity. They're inspiring because of their still-untarnished hopes and dreams. They're exciting because they're not afraid of the future, and they're bubbling over with brave new plans for a brave new world. With all this going for them, why do they have such a bad "image"? Why do so many people seem to think that ALL teens have bad habits and bad morals, use drugs and use parents, approve of free love and a free ride, and are going to ruin the world as soon as they get their hands on it? I'm PROUD of much of today's youth — and I want you to be, too.

I want you to give teens your concern instead of criticism, to build them up instead of always putting them down, and to teach them about me and my laws and my love.

But maybe you should try to think of some other way to bolster the upholstery in your VW — before you turn it into a petunia patch. That just may be a teen idea whose time has not yet come.

God

Dear God,

I am learning sign language. And I don't know if this is a good sign or a bad sign or just a sign of the times. Everywhere I look, there is a sign telling me to do something, go somewhere, don't do something, buy something, be something, know something, or wonder about something.

And you know something? Signs can be misleading — even road signs. Have you ever tried to watch the traffic, watch the road, and still read all those signs leading to complicated cross-over cloverleafs? You can end up headed toward the wrong city before you can say "Golly Ned," "Gee whiz," or "Dagnab it."

Right in our own neighborhood the post office has an interesting sign posted by the exit lane. It says "BEWARE! Mail Trucks." You're almost afraid to approach the exit lane, for fear a crazed, foaming-at-the-gas-tank mail truck will come racing out and attack you.

At the other extreme, I once saw a little hand-lettered sign in a front yard, warning trespassers about the dog that lived there.

Instead of saying "BEWARE OF THE DOG," it simply warned "Cross Dog."

I even have some signs of my own in my kitchen. One says "A messy house is a sign of character — wait till you meet the one who lives here!" The other sign says, "Incredible as it seems, my life is based on a true story."

Now THOSE signs are real and true. They tell it like it is.

But God, the signs I'm worried about are the ones that lure us to buy things we don't need, yearn for things we can't have, question things that should be absolute, and accept things that should be questioned. What do you think about all our signs today, God? How can I avoid them — so I won't always think I should be signing up or signing out?

Signing Off

Dear Signing Off,

I think that signs are necessary — and important. But you do have to learn to be discerning about which ones you will believe or follow.

I know I leave signs everywhere all the time — and people pass right by without ever seeing or believing them.

Instead of billboards, every spring I use flowering trees and bushes to proclaim my message of "new life" and my promise of eternal life. Instead of road signs, I left Ten Commandments. Instead of using cartoons, I use real people — and shine forth from them, hoping others will see and hear and understand.

So, Signing Off, look for MY signs — and when you are worried about what sign to follow or believe, remember there is one sign you can always follow and believe — the sign of the cross.

God

Dear God,

They say that mirrors don't lie — but that's a lie. I know because I have an untruthful mirror.

You should see the way I look in the mirror in my back bedroom. The way the light hits that mirror it accomplishes the same effect as those filters they put over a movie camera lens to make an aging screen star look younger.

Every morning that mirror tricks me into thinking I look terrific, and I leave the house thinking all's right with the world.

Ten minutes later I'm at the grocery and catch a glimpse of myself in the mirror over the meat counter. Somehow I've suddenly aged ten years. The meat mirror speaks the truth.

What should I do, God? Should I stay out of the back bedroom and join the meat cutters union so I can spend more time at the meat counter? Should I try to fool myself into thinking what I see in the bedroom mirror is the real me? Or should I become a surgeon or a bank robber so I can wear a mask over my face?

Trying to Save Face

Dear Trying,

It's unhealthy to spend too much time in front of a mirror. You become either vain or depressed. But it IS a good idea to look at yourself carefully and take stock once in a while.

Maybe you DO need a new diet, a new outfit, a new wrinkle cream (the face you save should be your own!). And after you've made improvements, maybe you'll like yourself better — and then everybody else will too.

In the same way, it's a good idea to take a long look into your spiritual mirror once in a while. It's all too easy to see yourself in the wrong light when it comes to religion, too. It's easy to overlook that little wrinkle of gossip or uncharitableness, that extra pound of intolerance, that midriff bulge caused by too little spiritual exercise.

So, Trying, keep on trying. Save your face as long as you can, but then forget it and don't worry about it anymore. Remember, the only important thing to save is your soul.

God

Dear God,

Why do you let children grow up when we're not looking? Isn't there a better way you could arrange that?

I think I first realized this one day when my son was about twelve years old. I was getting ready to go to a luncheon and I heard the kitchen door open, so I knew he had gone out into the garage. Within one minute I heard loud desperate shouts and wails. I couldn't imagine what great catastrophe could have occurred in the garage, but I went running to see.

There he stood, blood gushing out of his knee. He was wearing shorts, and as he had walked past my car somehow he had managed to make contact between his naked knee and the license plate. The sharp edge of the plate had sliced his knee like a knife. Who would have ever imagined that an innocent license plate on a car sitting quietly in the garage could be a safety hazard and a lethal weapon?

As I was wrapping his bleeding knee in my best towel (which, naturally, was the first thing I had grabbed — instead of an old one)

I muttered a suggestion that he stop bleeding until after the luncheon. Luckily, he didn't hear that since he was too busy moaning and worrying about all the ball games and swim parties he was going to miss.

I raced to the hospital and left him at the emergency room door, in the care of a nurse, while I went to park the car. By the time I dashed back from the parking lot he had already been whisked into a treatment room. The nurse told me to just take a seat in the waiting room. The WAITING ROOM? I had always been with my little boy in emergencies. But I meekly sat down and pondered the fact that although he was only twelve, he was already getting close to six feet tall while I was still tiptoeing to try to reach past five feet — so I guess they figured they could get along without me.

As I sat pondering and trying to read a magazine, I heard a voice on the intercom say, "Would the party with Mr. Snyder please come to the front desk." At first, it didn't register. The PARTY WITH MR. SNYDER? Was this a restaurant or a hospital? The PARTY WITH MR. SNYDER? Was I that party?

What had happened to the indispensable MOMMY? What had happened to the Mommy who stemmed the flow of blood, bandaged the bruises, soothed the fevered brow, and kissed it to make it well? Had she suddenly lost all her identity and become only the PARTY WITH MR. SNYDER?

I staggered to the desk and signed the insurance form the nurse handed me. She told me my son was all stitched up, and they didn't need anything else from me because he had given them all the information they needed and I could pick him up at the side door.

It was all over. My little boy had grown up while I wasn't looking. Why did you let that happen, God? Why do you keep doing this to unsuspecting parents?

Party of the Unsuspecting

Dear Party,

Time flies when you're raising children. But do you remember when you used to wonder if he would EVER be old enough to learn to walk . . . EVER be old enough to stop using baby talk . . . EVER be old enough to go to school, to ride his two-wheeler without training wheels, to stay alone without a sitter? Well, while you were wondering he was growing, and all of a sudden he was old enough.

Even parents who pay close attention are always surprised at how slowly the years seemed to go when they were living them and how fast they went when they look back. Only then do they think of all the things they wish they had done or said or celebrated.

So, Party of the Unsuspecting, don't let it happen again. Don't just plan to do things with the family IN THE FUTURE. Do things now. Enjoy today. Celebrate this day, this age, this opportunity. Today is the only tomorrow you truly have.

God

Dear God,

I just got back from a house tour, and now I have this terrible problem. My whole body has turned green with envy. Today we visited homes that had ''dreams come true'' features — an indoor swimming pool just off the kitchen! . . . stained glass windows and an Oriental rug in the bathroom . . . a combination breakfast room/greenery full of blooming plants and overlooking an elaborate garden . . . a child's sunny room with a canopied bed, antique furniture, and no toys out of place, no dirty clothes on the floor! I mean these houses even had plenty of closet space and windows that had been washed! Do you see why I'm depressed, God?

To make it even worse, all the women who went on this tour were dressed like fashion plates. Watching them step off the tour buses was like watching a commercial for a French fashion designer. And then, the lunch we were served included little finger sandwiches, fancy cookies, and a dainty elegant salad. Not a jar of peanut butter or catsup in sight!

When I hobbled home and told my husband about my exciting but depressing day, he said, "Why do you torture yourself by going to see those fancy houses when you know you have to come home to this one?" Without thinking, I replied, "Well, I enjoy going to see Paul Newman movies, but I still come home to you."

He did not think that was funny. Now I am facing two terrible problems — terminal envy and divorce court.

What should I do?

It's Not Easy Being Green

Dear Green,

Sorry to hear you have another outbreak of foot-in-mouth disease. Surprise your husband with a nice steak dinner tonight, and casually mention that you read where Paul Newman has gone into the salad dressing business and that he'll never seem romantic to you anymore — now that he has his picture on a salad dressing bottle. Maybe this will make your husband unpack his suitcase and put his lawyer on hold.

As for envy, that's a disease that's been around a long time — remember Cain and Abel and Joseph's brothers? No one's ever found a cure for this disease, but there IS an effective treatment. It's called COUNT YOUR BLESSINGS. Apply it daily, and it will gradually take that green tinge out of your complexion. You may still have occasional recurrences (if you visit the Hearst castle, the Vanderbilt mansion, or that neighbor down the street who just put in the solar greenhouse), but this potent remedy should make being green a little easier.

So don't be blue, Green. Even if you weren't "born to the purple," you have enough special riches of your own to keep you in the pink!

God

Dear God,

Well, today I did it! It wasn't easy. In fact, it took sheer willpower. It was a brave, courageous, heroic act. But I did it. I threw away my old, burnt, beat-up cookie sheet.

You know the one I mean, God — the one that looked like it had been through the War of 1812, the one I loved and used constantly. I had tried to ''dispose'' of it many times before, but I just couldn't get up enough courage to live without it. Finally, today when I heard the garbage truck coming up the street, I resolutely grabbed the cookie sheet, ran out the door, and stuck it in the garbage can. Within minutes the truck had come and gone, and it was too late to change my mind.

I may not win a medal for this act of bravery, but any homemaker would understand the seriousness of the situation and the ultimate fortitude required to perform such an act.

Maybe you haven't noticed, God, but there are an awful lot of homemakers just like me. We have a whole pantry full of pots and pans that look like they have just been retrieved from the side of a recently erupted volcano. Our skillets and saucepans are black and brown with blemishes of baked-on grease spots, dented and pockmarked, with handles that are a little loose and lids that don't fit quite right anymore. But we never seem to get around to trading them in on newer models — the ones that are bright and shiny, the ones with dainty painted-on flowers, the ones that are untouched by human homemakers engaged in daily kitchen battles.

Somehow we have the idea that these old war-torn utensils cook better. We are sure that the roast wouldn't taste the same if we used any other pot . . . the stew wouldn't simmer in the same way . . . the pancakes wouldn't turn golden brown . . . and the chicken wouldn't straighten up and fry right!

Maybe we subconsciously think that these old skillets and stewpots are symbols of all the years of time and trouble we have put into turning out meals that disappear within seconds — with no proof of the pudding left, no measure of the delicate measuring of spices and "secret ingredients," no masterpiece of our art left to hang on the wall or decorate the front hall.

Well, whatever the psychological reason behind it, God, I hung onto the cookie sheet too long. Today after I threw it out, I HAD to go out and buy a new one so I could bake the cookies I had promised for the school picnic. And you know what, God, the cookies baked as well as ever, just as golden, just as perfect as before. Now I am wondering why I hung onto that old, disgusting-looking, greasy cookie sheet all these years. Why, God, why?

Belated Bravery

Dear Belated Bravery,

Well, instead of a security blanket, you had a security sheet — and one that turned out terrific cookies. So don't feel TOO bad, B.B. I HAVE noticed there are a lot of homemakers like you — who have spotless kitchens that are cozy and bright with hanging baskets of flowers and pretty ruffled curtains and cabinets full of the WORST looking pots and pans imaginable.

Of course, appearance isn't everything. Some things that LOOK good aren't. So don't think you have to get rid of ALL your pots and pans — OR friends — just because they've gotten old and ugly!

But now that you've won the Kitchen Medal of Honor for trashing the cookie sheet, maybe it IS time to go through your cabinets — and your life — to see what you should throw out and what you should keep.

Once you really looked at that cookie sheet, you saw how disgusting it was — and you got rid of it. Maybe it's time you did the same thing with some of your old ugly habits.

You can do it. Because you're brave, courageous, and heroic — and I am with you all days, even to the end of your bad habits.

God